Sing-Along Holiday Stories

THE THIRTEEN DAYS OF HALLOWEEN

By Carol Greene

Illustrations by Tom Dunnington

CHILDRENS PRESS, CHICAGO

This book is for Rachel

Library of Congress Cataloging in Publication Data

Greene, Carol.
   The thirteen days of Halloween.

   (Sing-along holiday stories)
   Summary: Halloween version of "The Twelve Days of
Christmas," featuring such seasonal gifts as bats,
goblins, spiders, worms, and ghosts.
   1. Children's songs—United States. [1. Halloween—
Songs and music. 2. Songs] I. Title.
PZ8.3.G82Th   1983   784.6'2405   83-7347
ISBN 0-516-08231-0

On the first day of Halloween,
my good friend gave to me
a vulture in a dead tree.

On the second day of Halloween,
my good friend gave to me

two hissing cats
and a vulture in a dead tree.

On the third day of Halloween,
my good friend gave to me

three fat toads,
two hissing cats,
and a vulture in a dead tree.

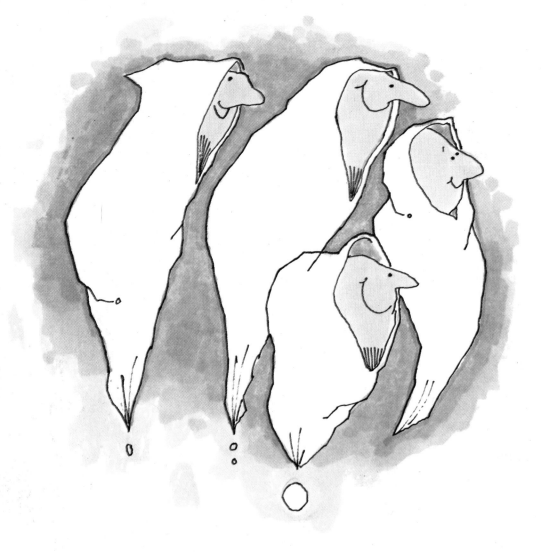

On the fourth day of Halloween,
my good friend gave to me
four giggling ghosts,

three fat toads,
two hissing cats,
and a vulture in a dead tree.

On the fifth day of Halloween,
my good friend gave to me
five cooked worms,

four giggling ghosts,
three fat toads,
two hissing cats,
and a vulture in a dead tree.

On the sixth day of Halloween,
my good friend gave to me
six owls a-screeching,
five cooked worms,

four giggling ghosts,
three fat toads,
two hissing cats,
and a vulture in a dead tree.

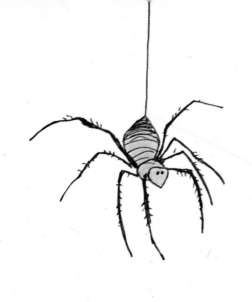

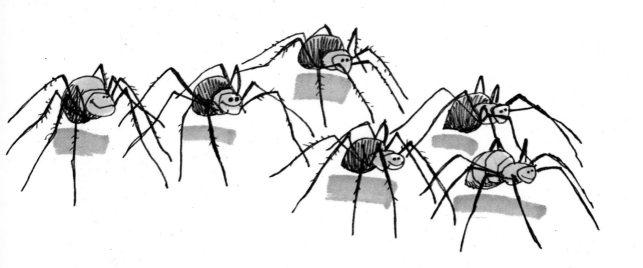

On the seventh day of Halloween,
my good friend gave to me
seven spiders creeping,
six owls a-screeching,

five cooked worms,
four giggling ghosts,
three fat toads,
two hissing cats,
and a vulture in a dead tree.

On the eighth day of Halloween,
my good friend gave to me
eight brooms a-flying,
seven spiders creeping,
six owls a-screeching,

five cooked worms,
four giggling ghosts,
three fat toads,
two hissing cats,
and a vulture in a dead tree.

On the ninth day of Halloween,
my good friend gave to me
nine wizards whizzing,
eight brooms a-flying,
seven spiders creeping,

six owls a-screeching,
five cooked worms,
four giggling ghosts,
three fat toads,
two hissing cats,
and a vulture in a dead tree.

On the tenth day of Halloween,
my good friend gave to me
ten goblins gobbling,
nine wizards whizzing,
eight brooms a-flying,
seven spiders creeping,

six owls a-screeching,
five cooked worms,
four giggling ghosts,
three fat toads,
two hissing cats,
and a vulture in a dead tree.

On the eleventh day of Halloween,
my good friend gave to me
eleven bats a-swooping,
ten goblins gobbling,
nine wizards whizzing,
eight brooms a-flying,

seven spiders creeping,
six owls a-screeching,
five cooked worms,
four giggling ghosts,
three fat toads,
two hissing cats (pant, pant),
and a vulture in a dead tree.

On the twelfth day of Halloween,
my good friend gave to me
twelve cauldrons bubbling,
eleven bats a-swooping,
ten goblins gobbling,
nine wizards whizzing,
eight brooms a-flying,

seven spiders creeping,
six owls a-screeching,
five cooked worms,
four giggling ghosts,
three fat toads,
two hissing cats (I think I'm going to faint),
and a vulture in a dead tree.

On the thirteenth day of Halloween,
I invited my good friend to lunch

and gave HER a present,
a real, live. . .

guess what.

The Thirteen Days of Halloween

Carol Green

Old English Song

6. On the sixth
7. On the seventh
8. On the eighth
9. On the ninth   } day of Hal-low-een my good friend gave to me:
10. On the tenth
11. On the eleventh
12. On the twelfth

six   owls a-screech-ing
seven spiders creep-ing
eight brooms a-fly-ing
nine   wizards whiz-zing } five cooked worms, four giggling ghosts,
ten   goblins gob-bling
eleven bats a-swoop-ing
twelve cauldrons bub-bling

three fat toads, two his-sing cats, and a vulture in a dead tree.

(The thirteenth day doesn't have a tune.)

About the Author

Carol Greene has a B.A. in English Literature from Park College, Parkville, Missouri and an M.A. in Musicology from Indiana University, Bloomington. She's worked with international exchange programs, taught music and writing, and edited children's books. She now works as a free-lance writer in St. Louis, Missouri and has had published over 20 books for children and a few for adults. When she isn't writing, Ms. Greene likes to read, travel, sing, and do volunteer work at her church. Her other books for Childrens Press include: *The Super Snoops and the Missing Sleepers; Sandra Day O'Connor: First Woman on the Supreme Court; Rain! Rain!; Please, Wind?; Snow Joe;* and *The New True Book of Holidays Around the World.*

About the Artist

Tom Dunnington divides his time between book illustration and wildlife painting. He has done many books for Childrens Press, as well as working on textbooks, and is a regular contributor to *Highlights for Children.* Tom lives in Oak Park, Illinois.